First Facts®

SOIL, SILT, AND SAND

LAYERS OF THE UNDERGROUND

by Jody Sullivan Rake

Consultant:
Susanne Clement, PhD
Assistant Professor, Department of Geology
Kent State University
Kent, Ohio

CAPSTONE PRESS
a capstone imprint

First Facts are published by Capstone Press,
1710 Roe Crest Drive, North Mankato, Minnesota 56003
www.capstonepub.com

Library of Congress Cataloging-in-Publication Data
Rake, Jody Sullivan, author.
  Soil, silt, and sand : layers of the underground / by Jody Sullivan Rake.
      pages cm. — (First facts. Underground safari)
  Summary: "Teaches readers about layers and types of soil, dirt, and earth underground"—Provided by publisher.
  Includes bibliographical references and index.
  ISBN 978-1-4914-5063-5 (library binding)
  ISBN 978-1-4914-5093-2 (eBook pdf)
1. Soil ecology—Juvenile literature. 2. Soils—Classification—Juvenile literature. 3. Soils—Juvenile literature. I. Title.
  QH541.5.S6R35 2016
  577.5'7—dc23
                            2015000587

Editorial Credits
Abby Colich, editor; Heidi Thompson, designer; Jo Miller, media researcher Katy LaVigne, production specialist

Photo Credits
Alamy: Photoshot Holdings Ltd/Photos Horticulture/Michael Warren, 9 (inset); Capstone Studio/Karon Dubke, 21; Newscom: Charles O. Cecil/Danita Delimont Photography, 17, Mopic Science Photo Library, 19; Science Source: Nigel Cattlin, 11; Shutterstock: Alain PITAULT, 7, Creative Nature Media, cover (middle), 9, dan_nurgitz, 7 (inset), Kichigin, cover (background), KRUKAO, 2, Raduga11, cover (left), 13, 15, SCOTTCHAN, 2, udra11, 5, underworld, cover (right)

Design Elements
Shutterstock: Hal_P, LudmilaM

Printed in China by Nordica
0415/CA21500544
042015   008845NORDF15

TABLE OF CONTENTS

SOIL IS LIFE!

Soil is more than dirt you wash off your hands. Soil is needed for life! Almost all plants grow in soil. Plants get *nutrients* from soil. Many creatures also live in soil.

Soil is made of many things. It is mostly made up of tiny bits of rock. Besides rock, soil contains tiny bits of dead plants and animals. These bits of dead life are called *organic* matter.

nutrient—a substance needed by a living thing to stay healthy
organic—part of an animal or plant

DIG IN!

Even tiny bits of bone make up the organic matter in soil.

KINDS OF SOIL

Three kinds of rock pieces are found in soil—sand, silt, and clay. The largest rock pieces in soil are sand. If you've ever been to a beach or desert, you've seen sand. Water drains quickly through sand, making it difficult for plants to grow. Only plants that need very little water can grow in sand.

sand bits

Silt bits are 100 times smaller than sand bits. The bottom of a lake or pond contains soil that is mostly silt.

Clay pieces are the smallest bits found in soil. They are 1,000 times smaller than sand. Clay pieces are too tiny to see with your eyes. They are closely packed together. Water has a hard time getting through. Nothing can grow in pure clay.

clay soil ▶

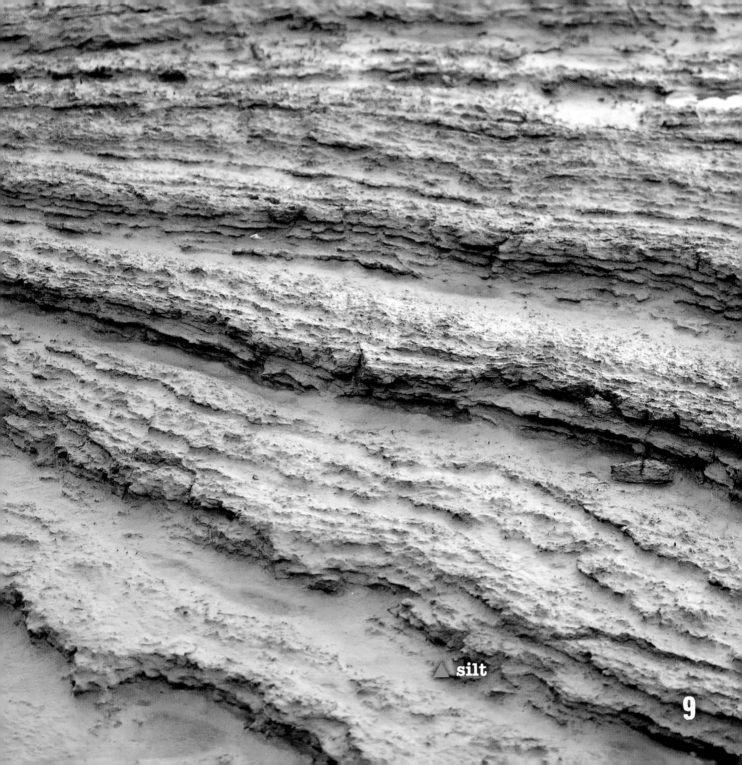

△ silt

9

LOAM, SWEET LOAM

Loam is a type of soil. Loam is made of nearly equal parts sand, silt, and clay. Loam usually holds just the right amount of water. It is the best type of soil for growing plants. Loam is usually near the top of the ground. It can be found on farms where food is grown.

loam—rich soil that is made up of sand, clay, and silt

▼ loam soil

11

THE LAYERS BELOW

The ground under your feet is made up of layers. Soil comes first. The top layer of soil is called *topsoil*. Topsoil is where plant roots grow and many animals live.

Under the topsoil is a layer of *subsoil*. Subsoil contains more clay and rocks, and less organic matter than topsoil. Very few animals and almost no roots are in subsoil.

DIG IN!

Layers of soil are called horizons.

topsoil—the layer of soil in which plants grow
subsoil—a layer of rock or soil beneath the surface of the ground

ROCK BOTTOM

Below the subsoil is a layer of rock. The top part of this layer is called parent material. Parent material breaks into smaller pieces to form soil. You would find little or no organic matter here.

Beneath the parent material is a layer called *bedrock*. Parent material comes from the same rock as bedrock. Bedrock may stay buried and hidden for hundreds of years.

bedrock—a layer of solid rock beneath the layers of soil and loose rock

bedrock

DIG IN!

Sometimes an earthquake causes deep cracks in the earth. Bedrock can be seen in the cracks.

WATER UNDER THE GROUND

Massive amounts of water can be found under the ground. How did it get there? Water from rainfall, lakes, and rivers seeps into the ground. It keeps going until it hits bedrock. Water remains underground in *aquifers*. People can reach this water by digging wells.

DIG IN!

There is 100 times more water in the ground than in all the earth's lakes and rivers!

aquifer—an underground body of water

▲ women getting
water from a well
in Senegal

TO THE CENTER OF THE EARTH

All the layers of soil and rock are part of Earth's *crust*. Beneath the crust is a very deep layer called the *mantle*. The mantle is made of mostly solid rocks and *minerals*. Beyond the mantle at the very center of Earth is the *core*. The outer core is super hot liquid *iron*. The inner core is solid.

crust—the thin outer layer of Earth's surface
mantle—the layer of super hot rock that surrounds Earth's core
mineral—a material found in nature that is not an animal or a plant
core—the inner part of Earth that is made of iron
iron—a very hard metal

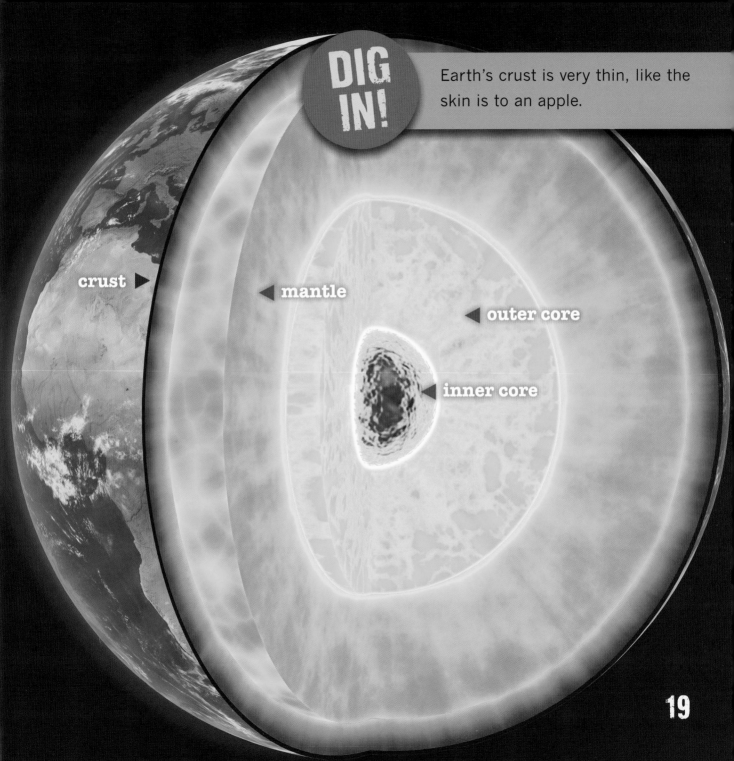

DIG IN!

Earth's crust is very thin, like the skin is to an apple.

crust ▶

◀ mantle

◀ outer core

◀ inner core

DON'T HURT THE DIRT!

Soil is important to life. We need to protect it. Food, paper, and even your clothes come from plants that grow in soil. Never *litter* the soil or *pollute* it in other ways. We need to take care of soil so it can take care of us!

litter—to throw garbage on the ground
pollute—to make something dirty or unsafe

aquifer (AK-wuh-fuhr)—an underground body of water

bedrock (BED-rahk)—a layer of solid rock beneath the layers of soil and loose rock

core (KOR)—the inner part of Earth that is made of iron

crust (KRUHST)—the thin outer layer of Earth's surface

iron (EYE-urn)—a very hard metal

litter (LIT-uhr)—to throw garbage on the ground

loam (LOHM)—rich soil that is made up of sand, clay, and organic matter

mantle (MAN-tuhl)—the layer of super hot rock that surrounds Earth's core

mineral (MIN-ur-uhl)—a material found in nature that is not an animal or a plant

nutrient (NOO-tree-uhnt)—a substance needed by a living thing to stay healthy

organic (or-GAN-ik)—part of an animal or plant

pollute (puh-LOOT)—to make something dirty or unsafe

subsoil (SUHB-soyl)—a layer of rock or soil beneath the surface of the ground

topsoil (TAHP-soyl)—the layer of soil in which plants grow

Nemeth, Jason. *Earth's Layers*. Our Changing Earth. New York: PowerKids Press, 2012.

Spilsbury, Richard and Louise. *Soil*. Let's Rock. Chicago: Heinemann, 2011.

Walker, Kate. *Soil*. Investigating Earth. New York: Marshall Cavendish Benchmark, 2012.

INTERNET SITES

FactHound offers a safe, fun way to find Internet sites related to this book. All of the sites on FactHound have been researched by our staff.

Here's all you do:

Visit *www.facthound.com*

Type in this code: 9781491450635

 Super-cool stuff! Check out projects, games and lots more at **www.capstonekids.com**

CRITICAL THINKING USING THE COMMON CORE

1. Name two things that make up soil. (Key Idea and Details)

2. Choose two kinds of soil to compare and contrast. How are they different and similar in how they look? How do they differ in how well they can grow plants? (Craft and Structure)

3. Reread page 20. What would happen if all the soil in your area was damaged and couldn't grow plants? Support your answer. (Integration of Knowledge and Ideas)

INDEX